THE
JOY
OF
NO

THE JOY OF NO

An Hachette UK Company
www.hachette.co.uk

Summersdale Publishers Ltd
Part of Octopus Publishing Group Limited
Carmelite House
50 Victoria Embankment
LONDON
EC4Y 0DZ
UK

www.summersdale.com

Printed and bound in Malta

ISBN: 978-1-78685-949-5

Substantial discounts on bulk quantities of Summersdale books are available to corporations, professional associations and other organisations. For details contact general enquiries: telephone: +44 (0) 1243 771107 or email: enquiries@summersdale.com.

THE
JOY
OF
NO

#JONO

summersdale

Saying 'no' does not always show a lack of generosity and...

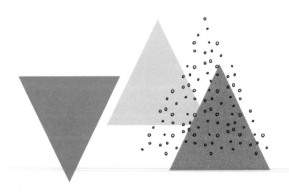

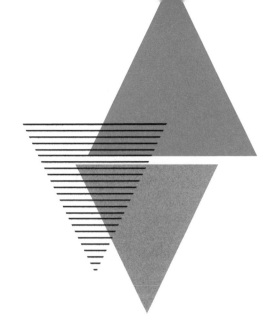

... saying 'yes' is not always a virtue.

Paulo Coelho

SAY 'YES' TO SAYING 'NO'

It's no surprise that the word 'no' has negative connotations – after all, it is literally the negative response to a question or request. But it's time we stop seeing it as a negative word and start embracing it for the joy, calm, space and positivity it can bring into our lives. We often have the best intentions when we say 'yes' to extra tasks at work, or to invitations to social events we don't really want to go to, but more often than not these encroachments into our time are actually causing more harm than good. Every 'yes' we don't really mean can invite resentment, poor-quality work, stress and exhaustion, and can set us up for failure. By saying 'no' to things we don't want to do or that don't benefit us, we make room for healthy and fulfilling relationships, for 'me time', for the headspace to actually get our lives in order and the satisfaction of knowing we've completed work to the highest level.

This book will help you find healthy boundaries and learn how to assert yourself when someone steps over them. It will teach you, practically, how to say 'no' in a world where we're conditioned to say only 'yes'. It will free you from all those niggling 'shoulds' in life – 'I *should* help out at the charity fundraiser'; 'I *should* meet up with that friend because I haven't seen her in months'; 'I *should* take on those extra tasks at work even though I don't have time.' It will help you streamline your life, leaving you with an abundance of time and energy for the things that bring you real joy.

So let's stop spreading ourselves too thin; stop trying to satisfy everyone and do everything; stop worrying about letting other people down, because a 'yes' you can't really fulfil with commitment is barely a 'yes' at all. Of course, we're not suggesting you start turning down every request posed to you, or start refusing to do your actual job, but there's something invigorating about knowing when to embrace the power of 'no'. Let's move past thinking of 'no' as a negative or limiting word. Think of it instead as your key to freedom.

KEY

The tips in this book are divided into categories to help you locate the ones that are most relevant to you. You'll see icons on each tip page. This is what they mean:

Practical advice – the 'how-to' tips you'll need to say your 'no's with confidence	Negativity – dealing with naysayers and soul-suckers	Social – navigating social events, big and small, and social anxiety
Family – how to handle your relatives	Friends – saying no to people you like	Home – chores, chores, chores
Work – managing your workload	Money matters – that most delicate of topics: finances	Say yes! – because life can't all be full of 'no's

I GIVE MYSELF PERMISSION TO SAY 'NO' TO THINGS I DON'T WANT TO DO.

TO SAY 'YES' OR 'NO': THAT IS THE QUESTION

How do you know when you should say 'no'? There are things to consider before you start breaking out your new, confident 'no's left, right and centre, but most of the time you'll be able to tell quickly whether a 'no' is the right way forward by the twisting of your gut when someone approaches you with a request. Most of the time you know instinctively how full your week is and how much pressure you're already under, and sometimes you'll just *really, really* be looking forward to a day with empty hours ahead of you. But it's helpful to take a few moments to really consider a few questions first, to set your priorities straight.

MY GOAL NOW IS TO... ONLY DO THINGS I LOVE, AND NOT SAY YES WHEN I DON'T MEAN IT.

SANDRA BULLOCK

Life shrinks or expands in proportion to one's courage.

Anaïs Nin

ASSESS YOUR PRIORITIES

In general, you need to be thinking about what, in life, means most to you. If you had no priorities or commitments, how would you fill your time? Who comes first – family, your partner, friends, work, fitness, your mental health... you? If your social life and personal well-being come top of the list and work is just a way of getting by, then you'll know that taking on extra work tasks or being sucked into activities with family that won't fulfil you will probably require a firm 'no'. If your work is your main passion in life and you're offered responsibilities that could really help boost your career prospects, or a project you'll find personally satisfying, then perhaps you can find some time for it; but a time-consuming request outside of work that'll encroach on your little free time will be a strong 'no'.

I WILL EMBRACE EVERY DAY OF MY LIFE.

YOU CAN BE A
GOOD PERSON
WITH A KIND
HEART AND
STILL SAY NO.

LORI DESCHENE

TAKE TIME TO CARE FOR YOURSELF

Set yourself some personal boundaries to take care of your mental health. In order to feel like a normal, fully functioning human being, how many evenings per week do you need to spend at home, or on your own, doing the things you love (even if that's sitting on the sofa with your favourite book or taking a leisurely stroll around the neighbourhood)?

It's perfectly acceptable to allocate time in your week where your only objective is 'to relax' – book the time into your diary and don't give it up because you feel it's not a 'real' excuse.

I AM STRONG,

CONFIDENT

AND POWERFUL.

YOUR TIME IS LIMITED, SO DON'T WASTE IT LIVING SOMEONE ELSE'S LIFE.

Steve Jobs

TRUST YOUR GUT

When faced with a decision, ask yourself the following questions: Do I have the time? Do I *want* to do this? Will it benefit me? Will I feel bitterness or resentment when doing it? What will I have to ditch to make time for this? Will it cause me extra stress? If I say 'yes', will I be looking to make excuses or to blatantly lie to get out of it at a later date? How will this affect my relationship with this person?

Once you've answered these questions honestly, you'll have your answer as to whether you should be saying 'yes' or 'no'. But it's easier said than done, so... how do you actually say 'no'?

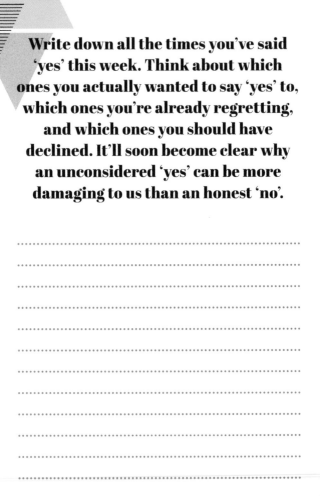

Write down all the times you've said 'yes' this week. Think about which ones you actually wanted to say 'yes' to, which ones you're already regretting, and which ones you should have declined. It'll soon become clear why an unconsidered 'yes' can be more damaging to us than an honest 'no'.

....
....
....
....
....
....
....
....
....
....
....
....
....
....

'NO' CAN BE A POSITIVE WORD.

WITH CONFIDENCE,
YOU HAVE WON
EVEN BEFORE YOU
HAVE STARTED.

Marcus Garvey

'NO' MAKES ROOM
FOR 'YES', AND WHO
DOESN'T WANT MORE
ROOM FOR THAT?

Kelly Corrigan

SAY 'NO' LIKE YOU MEAN IT

'Yes' is a lovely word. It slips off the tongue so easily, it makes the other person so happy, and it makes us feel like we're being nice, helpful and positive. But you can have that experience saying 'no', too. There are a variety of ways in which you can make your 'no' the most polite and helpful answer.

For instance, when you say 'no', make sure you mean it. Actually consider whether or not you can do what's being asked of you before giving an answer. Showing that you are not dismissing things too quickly helps the other person feel listened to and shows respect, and giving it due consideration means that you'll be known for only saying 'no' when there is no other answer.

Explain why you have decided to say 'no', if it's helpful. Telling the other person what you would be sacrificing in order to say 'yes' may help them see your point of view, but is by no means obligatory.

STAND YOUR GROUND

Don't give false hope by turning your 'no' into a 'maybe', or a 'no, but...' – once you have decided, the kindest thing is to stick to your answer and let them find someone else to step in. Let your decisions have integrity.

Don't dig yourself a hole. This is why it's easiest to just say 'no' – the more you keep talking out of guilt or a misplaced intention to make the other person feel better, the more likely you are to turn those 'no's into 'maybes', or 'I can't do that, but I could do this...' – which you more than likely still don't want to do. Give your answer, and then change the subject, or thank them for thinking of you, wish them the best and excuse yourself.

Don't give in to flattery! It's even harder to turn down a request when someone is telling you you're the *only* person for the job, you'd be *amazing* at it and they're desperate to have you on board. But if you've weighed it up and want to say 'no', they'll have to accept your answer.

Follow your honest convictions, and stay strong.

William Makepeace Thackeray

ONE OF THE SIMPLEST WAYS TO STAY HAPPY IS BY LETTING GO OF THE THINGS THAT MAKE YOU SAD.

ANONYMOUS

RESPECT YOUR DECISION

Ditch the guilt. For instance, if someone asks you to babysit at the last minute, but you had planned to go to the gym, it's not selfish to say 'no' – your commitment to a healthy lifestyle and to taking time for yourself and your hobbies, is important!

Depending on the situation, you may experience pushback to your newfound love of 'no's, but remember that anyone who does not respect your time, well-being or personal boundaries is maybe not someone you should be spending time with. If they keep pressing you for a 'yes', repeat your initial answer. Explain that you wouldn't be being fair to yourself and you'd be letting other people down if you said 'yes'. Stay calm, but hold your ground.

GETTING INTO THE 'POSITIVE NO' MINDSET

First things first: we know that saying 'no' isn't as easy as it sounds. And there are certain rules to be observed – responding to a polite request with an aggressive 'no' may not go down too well. But an assertive and reasonable 'no' *can* be a complete sentence: it just takes a little bit of getting used to. When it comes to actually delivering a 'no' in the real world, try to keep a positive mindset, and remember your 'no' is a positive step – not a problem. Speak with confidence, and let go of any guilt associated with the word. Stepping outside your comfort zone may be hard at first, but every time you try it, you'll increase your resilience and tolerance of any perceived discomfort, so practise it first. Try not to make the other person feel bad for asking, but offer an apology only if it's warranted and not by default; and remember that if the request was unreasonable in the first place you are not required to make excuses for turning it down.

RESPECT YOURSELF AND OTHERS WILL RESPECT YOU.

Confucius

SAYING 'NO' WITH CONFIDENCE

The key thing in delivering your 'no's is confidence. You can always pop to the bathroom for two minutes to get into the right mindset first! Stand in front of a mirror (preferably at home or in private) and strike a power pose. This involves standing tall, legs apart, back straight, chest wide and arms confidently by your side. Take up as much space as you can. No squirming or nervously crossed arms allowed. Take a few deep breaths and feel your confidence levels rising. Research from Harvard Business School has found that holding a pose like this for just two minutes boosts testosterone levels, which are associated with confidence, and decreases cortisol levels, which are associated with stress. Now say the word 'no' several times, slowly and calmly, in a strong but non-aggressive voice. It may naturally come out quietly at first, so practise making sure your voice is heard.

MOVE ON

There's so much angst and guilt associated with turning someone down that, even if you've managed to start saying 'no' to things, you may be plagued by worry – about being perceived as mean-spirited or unhelpful, or about what the person you turned down thinks of you. Or you may start to blow things out of proportion about how the other person will cope without your help. In reality, they probably barely registered your response because they had to move on and find someone else to pose their request to. You're very unlikely to lose a friend or risk missing out on a promotion just because you are realistic about what you can and can't do – in fact the person you turned down will probably respect you more. It's only you who is still worrying about it and wondering whether actually you could help them out if only you skip that family meal you've been looking forward to...

IF YOU ARE TOO BUSY TO LAUGH, YOU ARE TOO BUSY.

Proverb

Caring for myself is not self-indulgent. Caring for myself is an act of survival.

Audre Lorde

GET COMFORTABLE SAYING 'NO'

Saying 'yes' to things just to avoid feelings of guilt or awkwardness does a huge disservice to you, and doesn't help anyone in the long run. If you're always saying 'yes' to people, they'll always expect you to drop things for them and you'll find they respect your personal boundaries less and less as time goes on. Is your guilt or your 'yes' worth it when the request comes from someone who won't actually appreciate what it costs for you – especially when it comes with so few benefits and only temporary praise?

YOU REALLY
HAVE TO
LOVE
YOURSELF
TO GET
ANYTHING
DONE IN
THIS WORLD.

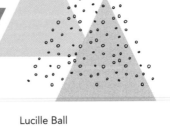

Lucille Ball

Very little is needed to make a happy life; it is all within yourself, in your way of thinking.

Marcus Aurelius

# DITCH THE GUILT

If accommodating everyone else's demands is leaving you feeling stressed, remind yourself that you can't please everyone all the time so there's no point worrying about it. You need to have the energy to look after yourself first before you can help others.

An over-stretched person on the edge is no help to anyone. If you had a friend who never bothered to look after themselves or who was feeling constantly under pressure, you would advise them to take some time off to look after themselves and recuperate. Why can't you do that for yourself? Saying 'no' gives you this space, so don't feel guilty about it – embrace it as a positive step towards a more rounded and fulfilled life.

YOU YOURSELF, AS
MUCH AS ANYBODY IN
THE ENTIRE UNIVERSE,
DESERVE YOUR LOVE
AND AFFECTION.

Anonymous

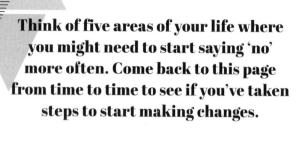

Think of five areas of your life where you might need to start saying 'no' more often. Come back to this page from time to time to see if you've taken steps to start making changes.

....

....

....

....

....

....

....

....

....

....

....

....

....

....

....

....

....

I DESERVE TO SURROUND MYSELF WITH PEOPLE WHO MAKE ME HAPPY.

SAY 'NO' TO SOUL-SUCKERS

Everyone knows one: that person who just drains your energy and leaves you feeling depleted. Whether you have to work with them or you're related to them, or you've just kept in contact with them out of habit, it's time to reclaim your positive vibes and put a strict limit on soul-sucking time. These situations can be tricky because most of the time you'll be turning down their invitations to protect your mental health and happiness, rather than because you have a prior commitment, which is often seen as a more acceptable excuse. But just because you don't have anything else on, it doesn't mean you *should* spend your time with someone who brings you down. Remind yourself what you'll be losing out on by saying 'yes' – even if it's just a matter of time, remember that that's still valuable.

HOW TO SAY 'NO'
TO SOUL-SUCKERS

When faced with a soul-sucker, a short and definite response is essential – you don't want to offer any leeway with a sympathetic look or an 'I'm really sorry'. They are bound to keep pressuring you if it's not an outright 'no'. Here are some things you can practise saying to the soul-suckers in your life next time they want something from you:

I'm flattered, but no thanks.

I have a full week this week so I've decided not to take on anything else.

I'm afraid I have new priorities so won't have time for this.

While the last time we worked together was great, I won't be doing that this time.

It's a shame, but I can't do that tonight.

A FRIEND IS SOMEONE WHO GIVES YOU TOTAL FREEDOM TO BE YOURSELF.

JIM MORRISON

MY TIME IS PRECIOUS: I WILL DECIDE HOW I SPEND IT.

IDENTIFYING TOXIC FRIENDS

Making time for your friends is essential to maintaining relationships, but do you ever wonder what you're getting out of a particular friendship? Spending quality time with friends who support you, make you feel loved and who you leave feeling happier and fulfilled is wonderful, but there are some friends who, for whatever reason, just bring you down. They may think they're being a great friend to you, but if you are constantly left feeling bad about yourself, anxious, depleted or just plain exhausted after spending time with them, it's time you put your own needs first and start minimising the time you spend with those negative people (or even cutting them out of your life altogether). Life is so short, and you should be prioritising *everything* – otherwise it'll run away from you and before you know it you'll have spent all your free time feeling rubbish in bad company. If you dread seeing a particular person, start saying 'no' to their invitations. See how much happier you become, and enjoy the buckets of time and energy you suddenly have left over for your true friends.

SAY 'NO' TO TOXIC FRIENDS

Saying 'no' does not make you a bad person, and being selective about who you spend your time with means you have more to give in the relationships that you do care about. It can be tricky, but making sure you're keeping yourself in a good headspace by reducing the time you spend with particular people will be more beneficial to you in the long run.

If you feel you just need to keep some distance from them for a while before reassessing the situation at a later date, here are some key phrases to have up your sleeve next time they ask you to hang out. Whether or not you give a reason or a hint as to where your head's at will depend on the person – be kind, but firm:

Thanks, but no thanks.

No, I have plans this week I'm afraid.

Sorry but I won't have any free time to hang out for a while.

Thanks for the invite, but I need some time to myself this week.

WHAT YOU DO TODAY CAN IMPROVE YOUR TOMORROWS.

RALPH MARSTON

Make a list of the people who bring you down and the people who raise you up. Some people may be somewhere in the middle – that's fine too. Just make sure none of them can get their hands on this book!

....

....

....

....

....

....

....

....

....

....

....

....

....

....

DO NOT FORGET YOUR DUTY TO LOVE YOURSELF.

Søren Kierkegaard

I DO NOT NEED TO WASTE TIME ON THOSE WHO BRING ME DOWN.

BREAKING UP WITH A TOXIC FRIEND

Friendships are constantly evolving. Even if someone has previously been a great, caring and respectful friend, if you're not getting what you need from them any more then you shouldn't feel bad about gently letting them go from your life. What you need today may not be what you needed when you first became friends. But it can be just as traumatic (if not more) to break up with a friend as it is to end a romantic relationship, so don't take the step lightly. If the other person is in need of support themselves, it may not be the kindest step to withdraw all friendship at once, particularly if they've been there for you in the past. If this person is normally supportive, perhaps they're just going through a rough patch. However, if they're someone who constantly demands your time and attention, brings unnecessary drama into your life, takes advantage of your good nature and who gives nothing in return, then perhaps it's time to move on completely. By cutting negativity from your life, you'll be saying 'yes' to true friends who make you smile, and who you know will be there to support you no matter what.

POSITIVITY IS THE WAY FORWARD.

TO LOVE ONESELF IS THE BEGINNING OF A LIFELONG ROMANCE.

Oscar Wilde

HOW TO BREAK UP WITH A TOXIC FRIEND

If you want to separate yourself from a toxic friendship, it can be tempting to just step back and wait for your friend to drift away. However, if they're not taking the hint, or if you feel you owe it to them to explain why you've made your decision, you may need to have a break-up conversation. Once you've decided you want to let go of a friendship, try writing down all your thoughts about the person so you can clarify your own reasons for ending the relationship. Perhaps you'll realise that they only ever talk about themselves, or that they are always negative, or they laugh when you tell them your dreams or talk about your feelings. You'll find it easier to have the conversation once you have clear reasons for why you're breaking up with them, regardless of whether you actually tell them or whether you spare their feelings with a softened version. You could write a script if it helps and practise saying out loud what you want to tell them.

HOW TO BREAK UP WITH A TOXIC FRIEND

Be direct and firm, but try not to offend them. You could say something general like, 'I don't feel like I'm getting what I need from you as a friend, so while I do care about you and I'm grateful for the friendship we've had, I think it's best we stop seeing each other.' Set clear boundaries if you need to, telling them that you don't want to hear from them again. If you have mutual friends, let them know that you're breaking off your friendship and try not to make things awkward for them by asking them to follow suit – you have to respect that while this person is no longer a great friend to you, they may still have a good relationship with other people.

I WILL FOLLOW

MY DREAMS.

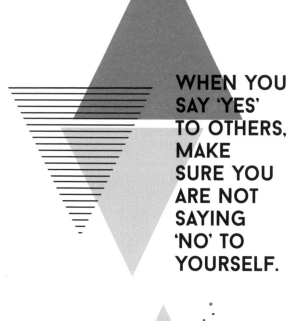

WHEN YOU SAY 'YES' TO OTHERS, MAKE SURE YOU ARE NOT SAYING 'NO' TO YOURSELF.

Paulo Coelho

QUICK WINS

Do you find your diary filling up weeks in advance with things you don't even really want to do? You've volunteered to help out at a friend's charity fundraiser, to babysit for a relative, to go to committee meetings or extra-curricular events, and to bake a cake for a colleague's leaving drinks. The free time you do have is somehow soaked up, leaving you feeling haggard and rushed off your feet. But how can you get out of these little niggling time-wasting activities that build up to rob you of your free time? Well there are some easy wins that can help: put a 'no junk mail' sign on your letterbox; unsubscribe from newsletters, magazines and catalogues (both online and physical); take your name off the committee list or ask to be relieved of any duties you have; buy a ready-made cake rather than baking one yourself.

 **QUICK WINS**

And then there's our buddy, 'no'. To all those little commitments and requests for 'quick favours', just say 'no'! This book could have been called 'be polite but firm' because that's the most important thing to remember, and it applies here more than anywhere. The phrase 'I have a busy week' can also be powerful tool here – there's no need to specify what you're doing, and most people will respect someone whose diary is full (they don't need to know it's full with taking a bath, having a date night with your partner, and sitting in the park in the sunshine).

TIME IS THE MOST VALUABLE THING A MAN CAN SPEND.

Theophrastus

Think of five small ways you could use 'no' in your life. How much more free time would this give you?

....

....

....

....

....

....

....

....

....

....

....

....

....

....

....

....

....

....

....

SAYING 'NO' IS NOT SELFISH.

SAYING 'NO' TO FAMILY

It's all well and good learning to turn down the odd invitation from a friend or a big project at work, but what about the people you can't pick? Those who, by blood, are part of your life, whose expectations of you often exceed those of your friends or colleagues. That's right: we're talking about your family.

Since expectations are higher, it can be harder for family to understand why you are turning down an invitation or request for help. They also know how to guilt-trip you into helping, and, as they also have the secret weapon of blood ties, they can dump their demands on you and know you're (probably) not going to walk away from them completely. But this arm-twisting and guilt-tripping to make you always say 'yes' can be exhausting, and by introducing a few more 'no's into your repertoire you'll make it clear that you are not a pushover and shouldn't be expected to be on-call for emergency taxi services or catering for Aunt Magda's annual Spring Fling.

SAYING 'NO' TO FAMILY

The first type of family 'no' to perfect is the 'No thanks, I don't want to come to/help organise another family event.' There are birthdays, engagement parties, weddings and anniversaries to be celebrated, and many more excuses for a party in between. Usually a 'thank you for the invitation but I'm busy that week' should be fine, but family are less afraid to pry into your personal business and demand explanations.

If you can't stand firm without giving an excuse, here's where white lies can be your friend. Hopefully your family are not *so* intrusive that they won't believe you have a prior work commitment or social engagement to attend.

Note: we don't condone lying in most situations, but if it helps ease the blow to your expectant Grandma then it's an acceptable diversion from the 'no-is-a-complete-sentence' rule. Try 'That's so lovely of you, but I've already planned X. Have fun though!' – and then change the subject before they can pry any further.

Is freedom anything else than the right to live as we wish? Nothing else.

Epictetus

I AM NEVER OBLIGED TO SAY 'YES'.

SAYING 'NO' TO FAMILY

Family also expect you to be at their beck and call whenever help is needed – to move house, give them a lift, lend them some money, be a last-minute plus-one, look after the dog or the baby or just to pop in to feed the cat. If it's something you've been known to help out with in the past, they may even jump straight to assuming you'll help out without even asking first – 'Oh you don't mind dropping that off at George's house for me, do you?' This is where you need to start putting your foot down and drawing a firm line to show your family where your boundaries are, and hope they understand and respect your decision.

"

HALF OF THE
TROUBLES OF THIS LIFE
CAN BE TRACED TO
SAYING 'YES' TOO
QUICKLY AND NOT
SAYING 'NO' SOON
ENOUGH.

Josh Billings

SAYING 'NO' TO FAMILY

The key with family is to stick to your guns, but you could soften the blow by offering an alternative. Here are some stock phrases to try:

I'm really not that comfortable looking after kids, so I won't be able to look after X any more. Why don't you try my friend's babysitter? I can give you their number.

I can't commit to that big a responsibility without compromising my other plans. I would happily help you with X, but this is asking too much.

I'm afraid I just don't have the spare time to help you out this time round, but I can ask around to see if anyone else can?

# SAYING 'NO' TO FAMILY

And finally, there's the specific kind of 'no' that's reserved solely for family, as they're the only people who ever do this: 'No thank you, I don't need your help with my party planning/the cooking/the decorating.' They always mean well, but having your mother-in-law insist on bringing a dish to your party that is never going to fit with your theme, or having them 'help' you decorate for an event by taking the décor back to 1955, is something else you may find yourself having to say 'no' to. Try a simple and to the point, 'Thank you for the offer but that is all taken care of', with no room for quibbling.

EVERYTHING MATTERS.
OUR TIME IS
PRECIOUS.

HENRY CLOUD

Think about the people who you love, but who sometimes ask too much of you, or who you struggle to say 'no' to. Write down your thoughts about how best you could approach them here.

....

....

....

....

....

....

....

....

....

....

....

....

....

....

....

....

YOU HAVE TO BE ABLE TO LOVE YOURSELF BECAUSE THAT'S WHEN THINGS FALL INTO PLACE.

VANESSA HUDGENS

SAYING 'NO' DOES NOT MAKE ME A BAD FRIEND.

SAYING 'NO' TO REAL FRIENDS

The guilt that often comes with saying 'no' to our friends can be even more intense than with anyone else – you don't want your friends thinking you don't like them, or that you're boring, a flaker, or unreliable. But if you don't take care of yourself and give yourself the downtime you need to function properly, what kind of a friend would you be anyway? If it helps to explain your reasoning to friends who usually demand a lot of your time, try telling them that you want to be there and to have fun with them, but in order to have the energy to be a good friend you need to put yourself first for a while – perhaps you've got an extra-busy schedule at the moment because of work or family commitments, or you are dedicating yourself to a new fitness regime, or you just want to spend a few more evenings at home doing whatever you fancy. Whatever the reason, they're bound to understand (they've probably felt the same way themselves from time to time!) and will appreciate your honesty. The time you *do* spend together will then be much more appreciated by you both.

WHAT PROGRESS, YOU
ASK, HAVE I MADE?
I HAVE BEGUN TO BE
A FRIEND TO MYSELF.

Hecato

YOU'RE PERFECT
WHEN YOU'RE
COMFORTABLE
BEING YOURSELF.

Ansel Elgort

SAYING 'NO' TO REAL FRIENDS

The trick to saying 'no' to your friends is to emphasise that old classic: it's not you, it's me. You may need to elaborate a little more on your reasoning than you would with other types of 'no', but you can still stay concise and honest if it works for you, and you shouldn't feel pressured into giving a reason if you don't want to. 'I wish I could but I can't today,' is a helpful line to have up your sleeve – no need to add an excuse, and it still implies that you appreciated the offer, but it's just not the right timing. Try adding a touch of humour to soften the blow if it feels right (responding to 'Do you want to come to my fancy dress party?' with a friendly 'No way! You know I hate fancy dress!' can often get the point across more efficiently than lengthy explanations, but won't always be appropriate!). Remember: saying 'no' does not make you a bad friend. Thank your friend for thinking of you, but stick to your guns.

SAYING 'NO' TO REAL FRIENDS

For friends asking you for assistance – maybe they want your help organising an event, they want your expertise on a project or are asking you to give them a lift – of course it's the kind thing to do to help if you can (you never know when you might need them to repay the favour). However, if they're constantly making demands or you just really don't have the time or energy to help on this particular occasion, make sure you put your 'no' first and foremost – and state it clearly before giving your reason. Make it clear you've given the matter consideration and come to a clear conclusion, so as not to invite any quibbling or 'friendly' coercion. 'I've decided' is a great phrase to throw in here – a true friend will respect your decision, no matter the reason. Or try 'I need to say no' with an optional 'because...' – this implies there are strong and valid reasons behind your response that your friend should accept. Who knows, you might also be doing them a favour – they may not have realised how much they needed some 'me time' too.

FOLLOW YOUR
OWN STAR.

Dante Alighieri

SAYING 'NO' TO REAL FRIENDS

Work out whether you actually want to go to an event or just feel that you should. Unless it's a special occasion for your friend and they really need your support, you shouldn't ever do something just because you feel obliged to – try saying 'I'd like to but it's just not possible' or some other variation that gives a firm but kind 'no'.

Sometimes the best way to say 'no' to a friend is to counter their offer with one of your own. By putting the request into your own terms and converting an unappealing offer into one you'd happily accept, you both win. Say someone asks you to help them move house, but you don't feel up to it. Why not say 'I can't help that weekend, but I could help you decorate the following weekend if you want help?' They'll see that you're not saying 'no' out of spite and that you're still trying to be helpful.

Turn off your phone for an entire evening (or weekend, if you dare). Write down some of the things you could do with all your free time instead.

....
....
....
....
....
....
....
....
....
....
....
....
....
....
....
....
....

I HAVE WHAT I CALL 'SHOULD-LESS' DAYS. TODAY IS A DAY WHERE THERE IS NOTHING I 'SHOULD' DO.

Ellen Burstyn

I AM GRATEFUL
FOR THE LIFE
I LEAD.

SAYING 'NO' TO SOCIAL INVITATIONS

If you're not in the right frame of mind, making small talk with people you barely know or trying to make out that you're having a whale of a time can be utterly exhausting, even for the most sociable of people. But how do you turn down invitations to social events that just aren't up your street without being labelled a party pooper or a bore?

Firstly, think about how many social engagements you feel comfortable attending every week (for some people it'll be three or four; for others even one a week can feel like a strain) and stick to it. Then allocate a particular day or days a week for social commitments. For everything else you can use the 'My diary is full this week' excuse (no one need know what it's full of). This way you can avoid wearing yourself out and your schedule will be clearer, leaving you feeling rejuvenated for the things you do decide to do.

Wherever you are - be all there.

Jim Elliot

I WILL NOT SAY 'MAYBE' IF I WANT TO SAY 'NO'.

SAYING 'NO' TO BIG NIGHTS OUT

Perhaps you're just not a party person, or maybe you hate big group social events and prefer to meet up with friends one-on-one or in smaller, more casual settings? If this sounds like you, then try inviting your friends along to your own low-key events – going to the cinema, cooking a meal together, going for a walk, or just meeting up during the day for a coffee instead of going for a big night out. You will get the benefit of their company but on terms that suit you, and you won't feel so bad when you tell them that you can't make it to their wild parties.

SAY 'NO' TO SOCIAL MEDIA

So, you've turned down some of the many unappealing invitations you've received and you finally have a blissful evening to yourself, free to do whatever you want and spend some quality restorative time alone. What will it be? A bubble bath and an early night with a good book? A long evening stroll? Or sitting on the sofa scrolling through Twitter until you realise it's 1 a.m. and you haven't even eaten yet? All too often you're sucked in before you know it, and all that precious downtime you worked so hard to preserve has gone down the social-media drain. Studies have shown that frequent checking of social media sites actually increases anxiety, depression and feelings of loneliness, and can even increase your risks of obesity, heart disease and cancer due to the hours of mindless sedentary scrolling. It is believed that most adults spend around ten hours a day looking at some form of screen, and you can bet that most of that time is not spent doing anything productive or healthy. It's time to reclaim your free time!

TELL ME, WHAT IS IT YOU PLAN TO DO WITH YOUR ONE WILD AND PRECIOUS LIFE?

MARY OLIVER

LIFE BEGINS AT THE END OF YOUR COMFORT ZONE.

Neale Donald Walsch

SAYING 'NO' TO SOCIAL MEDIA

Try keeping a log of how much time you actually spend on a screen (not including at work) for a week to get a realistic picture of how many hours you're losing to browsing. Then try reducing your screen time by half, and then perhaps by half again until you're using it more consciously and only when you really want to. You can get apps for your phone or tablet which log or restrict the amount of time you can look at certain sites, or you could even turn off your Wi-Fi connection in the evenings if you struggle to control your urges. You'll suddenly find yourself with real, valuable chunks of time to spend doing those 'me-time' activities you promised yourself and time to dedicate to the things that really enrich your life – going for a run, having a deep conversation with a loved one, or just embracing ten minutes of pure peace and quiet.

Write down five things you love to do – the things that make your soul happy – but that you never have time for. Tick off one thing each day this week.

....

....

....

....

....

....

....

....

....

....

....

....

....

....

....

....

THERE ARE SO MANY GREAT THINGS IN LIFE: WHY DWELL ON NEGATIVITY?

Zendaya

SAY 'NO' TO FOMO

Everyone knows that social media's glossy sheen isn't real life, and that just because someone continually posts jaw-dropping photos of their latest exotic holiday or pictures of their enviable body and post-workout smoothies, it doesn't mean their life is actually perfect. But it can still be hard not to believe – when you see that perfect loved-up photo with the hashtag #couplegoals – that they're really having all the fun in the world while you're sitting at home in your pyjamas on a Friday night. You might feel pressure to be seen to be doing fun, active things and present yourself as a social butterfly, but it's important to learn that FOMO (fear of missing out) is a fabrication created by social media. If Instagram didn't exist, you would never have been worried that you weren't eating at the most photogenic restaurants or felt that gut-wrenching loneliness at seeing a photo of your friends out having fun without you – you just wouldn't have known about them, probably until days later when the pang of emotion would be dulled to a shrug and an 'Oh well.'

SAY 'NO' TO FOMO

The easiest way to get rid of FOMO is to limit your exposure to social media, but if that's just not possible for you there are ways of saying 'no' to FOMO itself. The most effective way is to focus on your own life without any desire to share it with the world. Schedule in activities you love, surround yourself with your positive friends who make you feel good about yourself, and take some time out for solitude, even if it's just taking a walk around the park at lunchtime by yourself. Periods of solitude can build your emotional resilience, encourage self-reliance and a feeling of control, and help you stop and reflect on what matters most to you.

Make a point of noticing how you feel and of going about your day mindfully, appreciating the smaller things like the feeling of a hot shower or the smell of a great meal you've cooked yourself. Taking notice of sensations and emotions makes them more pronounced, so you can start to appreciate how wonderful your life is without having to photograph it or tell the social-media world all about it.

I HOLD THE KEY TO MY OWN HAPPINESS.

"

YOU'RE BRAVER THAN YOU BELIEVE.

A. A. Milne

# SAY 'NO' TO FOMO

It also helps to really stop and think about how people go about presenting their lives on social media. Have you ever been to a dull event and wished you were somewhere else for most of it, but still managed to take a pretty picture that makes out you were having the best time ever? The lives you see on your friends' profiles aren't always the truth, and they're almost definitely omitting lots of less-than-perfect photos, moments and entire days when they probably weren't having the best time ever. So next time you see a photo of that crazy night out that you missed, ask yourself: would you actually have enjoyed yourself if you were there? Is this an accurate representation of the whole night? Would a night out with friends have been better for your mental health than whatever you were doing instead? The answer to all of these questions is probably a resounding 'no'.

FOR EVERY MINUTE YOU ARE ANGRY, YOU LOSE SIXTY SECONDS OF HAPPINESS.

RALPH WALDO EMERSON

Don't count your days; make your days count.

Anonymous

SAY 'NO' TO DOING ALL THE HOUSEWORK

If you live with other people, you'll be aware that the division of housework is *never* equal. No matter what the household dynamics, one person will always end up doing the majority of the household chores, bill paying, food shopping, the cleaning, the laundry, the gardening or the emotional work of decision-making for the whole house. If that person is you, then it's time to delegate. If you find yourself spending hours clearing up after everybody or rushing around to make sure the house keeps running, you're taking on too much.

Reduce the toll of housework by breaking up each job and encouraging others in your house to help you out. Instead of doing a weekly deep clean, do little jobs often – wipe down the kitchen surfaces while you're waiting for the kettle to boil, or put on some upbeat tunes for ten minutes and have a quick blast of cleaning the bathroom.

EITHER YOU RUN
THE DAY OR THE
DAY RUNS YOU.

Jim Rohn

STAY STRONG AND BE YOURSELF! IT'S THE BEST THING YOU CAN BE.

Cara Delevingne

SAY 'NO' TO DOING ALL THE HOUSEWORK

Divide household tasks up equally (allowing for differing levels of difficulty – taking the bins out once a week is not the equivalent to washing up twice a day, seven days a week) and ask everyone in the house to take on a chunk that suits them. If someone really hates cleaning the toilet but is an awesome cook, why not let them take on the cooking and washing-up duties? Play up peoples' strengths ('You're just so great at organising meal plans!') and give them 100 per cent responsibility for their domain so they can take pride in their work and know that they're in control. Giving everyone specific jobs makes it clearer what is being asked of them rather than a general 'Please help me more around the house.' Make sure everyone has roughly the same share of the work so there'll be no bitterness over who does what. Swaps are allowed if two people end up with their least favourite job. The point is for everyone to chip in rather than for one person to be sorting out the entire house.

SAY 'NO' TO DOING ALL THE HOUSEWORK

Some people won't be happy with the idea of a housework rota, but it's not fair to expect one person to take on all the work. Be understanding – don't ask them to clean the whole bathroom the second they get in from a long day at work, or just before a big match they've been waiting to watch. Make sure you thank them for a job well done too – positive affirmation works wonders on even the most reluctant cleaner.

If you're still struggling to get other household members to help out, try adding in incentives, such as the rule that anyone who misses their chores has to buy the house dinner instead – they'll soon find the thought of folding the laundry much more appealing!

I KNOW MY BOUNDARIES AND I WILL ASSERT THEM.

Just saying 'yes' because you can't stand the short-term pain of saying 'no' is not going to help you do the work.

Seth Godin

SAY 'NO' TO WORK OVERLOAD

There's a toxic idea in some workplaces that if you always stay late, putting in hours of (probably unpaid) overtime and you are constantly, stressfully busy, you're somehow succeeding. This is just not true. Spending too much time working actually reduces our productivity and has negative effects on our health and mental well-being – you may be working longer but you're probably not working *better,* and you won't be doing anyone any favours. You should be able to comfortably complete your allocated tasks within the hours you are paid to do your job; otherwise, your employer needs to seriously assess your job description.

If you feel you're being asked to do too much work and you can't fit it into your work week, try talking to your boss or helpful colleagues about how best to streamline your work, or about delegating jobs that might be better done by someone else – it's OK to ask for help!

SAYING 'NO' TO EXTRA TASKS AT WORK

If you're asked to take on additional work, take a moment to assess the scope of what you're being asked to do. How long will it take, and are you capable of doing it well? How will it benefit you professionally – is it an engaging activity you'd be pleased to take on, or are you going to end up stressed and without any recognition of the extra hours put in? Of course, some workplaces need everyone to take on little extra jobs from time to time, but if you simply don't have the time to take on more, it's perfectly reasonable to say 'no'. When you've decided to say 'no' to a job, you can explain your reasoning clearly and fairly – saying 'I'd like to help, but I already have enough to do' should do the trick. Or you could always try negotiating – 'I can only do that if you do this for me', or 'I can do A, but not B. You'll have to find someone else to help with that.' Just make sure you're not caught later on taking long lunches or hanging around the staff room as if you've not got enough work to do!

THE ART OF LEADERSHIP IS SAYING 'NO', NOT YES. IT IS VERY EASY TO SAY 'YES'.

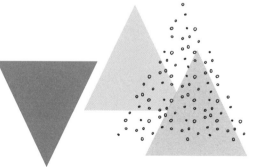

Tony Blair

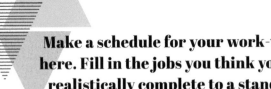

Make a schedule for your work-week here. Fill in the jobs you think you can realistically complete to a standard you're proud of. For anything that doesn't fit: delegate.

....

....

....

....

....

....

....

....

....

....

....

....

....

....

SAYING 'NO' TO YOUR BOSS

Saying 'no' to a superior at work can feel like a daunting task, but managers more than anyone should understand the importance of prioritising your workload. If anything, they are more likely to be impressed than cross because you're showing that you are aware of your limits and that you want to perform your job well. But if you have a boss who doesn't quite have this outlook, here are some phrases to try out next time they ask you to take on extra work that you can't fit in:

I don't have time to do that on top of my other work. Let me know if you'd like me to drop any other assignments to make room for this.

I could only take that on if I could delegate X to someone else.

Let me know if you'd like to go through my job description to see if we can reassess my workload.

I would not be able to take that on and deliver work I was proud of.

I WILL TAKE ON ONLY WHAT I CAN, AND I WILL GIVE EACH JOB MY ALL.

Think about the etiquette in your workplace. Are there particular people or policies that exacerbate the problem or create undue stress? Think about some practical solutions you could propose to your superiors here.

....

....

....

....

....

....

....

....

....

....

....

....

....

....

If you really want to be an effective time manager, you will have to learn to say 'no' to other people and do so frequently.

Sunday Adelaja

IF I AM NOT FOR MYSELF, NOT FOR MYSELF, WHO WILL BE FOR ME?

Hillel

I AM THE MASTER
OF MY FATE, I AM THE
CAPTAIN OF MY SOUL.

William Ernest Henley

SAY 'NO' TO GIVING YOUR TIME OR EXPERTISE FOR FREE

You're great at English, so all your friends ask you to proofread their CVs; you're good at maths, so everyone wants your help with their tax returns; you're creative, so people are always asking you to design their wedding invitations. There's always *something* that people assume they can demand of you simply because you're good at it. Sometimes there'll be the offer of 'great exposure' or publicity in exchange for it, but more often than not it's a thankless task with nothing in it for you. Unless you are going to be compensated for your time then you shouldn't give away your expertise for free. Even if your special skill is just a hobby, you've probably become good at it through years of practise, and that deserves to be acknowledged. Try something like 'I feel privileged that you thought of me but I don't offer my services for free. Good luck!' Sometimes the person is probably capable of doing the task themselves and just needs a bit of reassurance in their own abilities – 'I believe in you, you can do it!' may be just the push they need to stop relying on you as their security blanket.

WE ONLY GET ONE LIFE: LIVE IT WISELY.

A MAN WHO
DOES NOT THINK FOR
HIMSELF DOES NOT
THINK AT ALL.

Oscar Wilde

SAYING 'NO' TO PEER-PRESSURED SPENDING

Ah, money. We all need it – but it can cause so many problems and is one of the biggest sources of stress if we feel we don't have enough of it. Even worse is when you're trying to take control of your finances and have a 'sensible' month, and then a friend invites you on a big night out or to a new fancy restaurant, or all your friends decide to go on a trip that you just know will blow your budget out of the water. It can be really hard feeling like the party pooper by saying 'no', but you shouldn't feel afraid to stand your ground.

Most friends should be understanding if all you want to say is 'I can't afford to do that at the moment', but the pressure and the desire to keep up with the Joneses can feel quite intense. In these situations it's more to do with getting in the right frame of mind; you need to truly believe you are doing the right thing by turning an invitation down, and to try to ignore any feelings of missing out. Focus instead on what you really want, whether you are saving for something, or you just want to end the month without dipping into your overdraft for once. It can help to let all your friends know at the outset that you're trying to be frugal for a while, so they will know not to pressure you into things you can't afford. Ask for their support by not rubbing your face in the things you've missed, and try to pre-empt any feelings of FOMO by inviting them to do other, non-pricey activities, like having a night in watching your favourite film or playing games, or getting out into the country for a long walk instead.

Think of all the things you don't need to be doing that waste your valuable time and money, and list three things you're going to cancel this week.

....
....
....
....
....
....
....
....
....
....
....
....
....
....
....
....

FIND ECSTASY IN LIFE; THE MERE SENSE OF LIVING IS JOY ENOUGH.

EMILY DICKINSON

Every day brings new choices.

Martha Beck

EVERY MAN IS THE ARCHITECT OF HIS OWN FORTUNE.

APPIUS CLAUDIUS CAECUS

SAYING 'NO' TO LENDING MONEY

It's one thing to feel pressured into spending your money, but another one entirely to have to cope with friends who want to borrow it. This may not present a problem for some people, and it's great if you're in a position to help others without it affecting your own finances, but you could end up putting yourself into financial trouble by trying to always be the generous lender. It can even have long-term effects on your relationship: if one person begins to rely on you to help them out, denying them this can lead to resentment and bitterness on one side and guilt and shame on the other. When it comes to repeat-offender money scroungers, tell them gently that you don't think it's a good idea for friends to borrow money, and so you never lend money except in emergencies. If they don't get the hint, try taking cash with you when you go out and only taking enough for your own expenses so you can't possibly cover for them – they'll soon wise up.

SAYING 'NO' TO LENDING YOUR BELONGINGS

If it's your belongings someone wants to borrow (say they'd like to take your professional camera on holiday, or they'd like to borrow your car for a weekend) it can be easiest to simply tell them that some of your belongings are off-borrowing-limits. Rather than making them feel you don't trust them, make it clear that this is a general rule you have and isn't personal – 'I'm not comfortable lending my things' or 'I wish I could help but I have a rule never to lend my stuff' are useful phrases to have in stock.

I AM AN OASIS
OF CALM.

WHETHER YOU THINK YOU CAN OR YOU THINK YOU CAN'T, YOU'RE RIGHT.

HENRY FORD

SAYING 'NO' TO MONEY COLLECTIONS

A thoughtful leaving gift or birthday present from colleagues is a kind gesture but, unless you're loaded with cash, it can feel uncomfortable being pressured into donating a few pounds here and there; it all adds up, and not all of us *have* a fiver to give away at the drop of a hat. You don't want to look mean-spirited, but at the same time, perhaps that money was for your lunches for that week or pushes you into debt until payday. Etiquette writers Kim Izzo and Ceri Marsh say that 'a gift isn't a gift if it's an obligation', and nowhere is this more true than in the office collection for someone you barely know. If you're feeling bold, you can try just smiling and shaking your head when the collection comes round, or passing it on to the next person, but if you're pressed for an explanation there's no shame in saying you can't afford it this time round or saying you're giving them a card separately (but make sure you actually do it). This way it's clear you are doing your own thing and not just refusing to contribute.

Use this page to plan out your monthly budget, including the essentials (food, rent, bills), your regular outgoings (direct debits, nights out) and all your other outgoings (clothes, holidays, books etc.). See if you can find three things you can strike from this list to save money.

....
....
....
....
....
....
....
....
....
....
....
....

TAKE CARE OF YOUR BODY. IT'S THE ONLY PLACE YOU HAVE TO LIVE.

Jim Rohn

Don't waste a minute not being happy. If one window closes, run to the next window, or break down a door.

Brooke Shields

SAY 'NO' TO PEER PRESSURE

Even if you've said 'yes' to the event itself, social occasions can still be tricky to navigate – just because you want to go to the pub with your friends doesn't mean you want to get absolutely wasted, for instance. Peer pressure is something we think our friends will grow out of as we move on from our teenage years, but it can be a real challenge at any time. Sometimes white lies can be your friend here – 'I can't drink tonight because I've got an event in the morning I need to be fresh for' can be effective. But you may feel more comfortable just telling the truth: it just takes a bit of courage. Know you're not alone, and you're not the first person who has wanted to socialise without drinking/taking drugs/eating junk food/gambling or any of a host of other behaviours. Say 'no' confidently, and show that you have made your decision and intend to stick with it. If your friends continually refuse to respect your decision to abstain from any of the activities they're proposing, it may be part of a bigger problem with your friendships that needs to be addressed.

I AM THE ONLY PERSON WHO KNOWS WHAT'S BEST FOR ME.

HAVE RESPECT FOR
YOURSELF, AND
PATIENCE AND
COMPASSION. WITH
THESE, YOU CAN
HANDLE ANYTHING.

Jack Kornfield

SAY 'YES' TO THE THINGS THAT FULFIL YOU

This book has hopefully given you the confidence to say 'no' to the things you don't want to do, but life shouldn't all be about 'no's! There's a delicate balance between making a stand against unfair behaviours and just saying 'no' because you can. While it's helpful to have the experience of saying 'no' – and the ability to say it with confidence when appropriate – make sure you don't over-use it and miss out on opportunities. Life is short, so make sure you say 'yes' to doing the things you enjoy, and schedule in regular fun activities that you know you find fulfilling, with people who lift you up and support you. Once you've found the joy of saying 'no', you'll find that the joy of saying 'yes' when you truly mean it increases tenfold. So book in that poker night or hiking trip or pampering session or evening class or dinner with old friends, or that holiday you've always wanted to take, and embrace the joy of saying 'yes'.

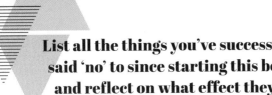

List all the things you've successfully said 'no' to since starting this book, and reflect on what effect they've had on your life. What else will you say 'no' to in future?

....
....
....
....
....
....
....
....
....
....
....
....
....
....
....
....

MOST PEOPLE ARE AS HAPPY AS THEY MAKE THEIR MINDS UP TO BE.

ANONYMOUS

LIFE IS EITHER A DARING ADVENTURE OR NOTHING.

Helen Keller

CONCLUSION

We hope this book has shown you that saying 'no' needn't be daunting or lead to feelings of guilt. When you've assessed a proposal and decided to turn it down, know that you're doing it for the benefit of your mental health and physical well-being. Putting yourself first every once in a while, is one of the most important things you can do. So ditch the guilt, and say 'yes' to 'me time' – enjoy your new-found freedom, productivity and healthy relationships. Find things that fulfil you, treat yourself to some quality alone time, and embrace the joys that saying 'no' can bring. Welcome to a new, assertive, positive and resilient you!

IT'S NOT SELFISH TO LOVE YOURSELF, TAKE CARE OF YOURSELF, AND TO MAKE HAPPINESS A PRIORITY. IT'S NECESSARY.

Mandy Hale

If you're interested in finding out more about our books, find us on Facebook at **Summersdale Publishers** and follow us on Twitter at **@Summersdale**.

www.summersdale.com

Image credits

Briefcase icon – pp.8, 119, 121, 124, 131 © Viktar Dzindzikav/Shutterstock.com

Chunky speech marks – pp.24, 41, 74, 83, 88, 104, 108, 113, 130, 152, 157 © TIP TOP/Shutterstock.com

Family icon – pp.8, 69, 70, 73, 75, 76 © Rauf Aliyev/Shutterstock.com

Home icon – pp.8, 112, 115, 116 © veronchick84/Shutterstock.com

Lightbulb icon – pp.8, 13, 16, 19, 25, 26, 29, 30, 33, 34, 37 © Vector Market/Shutterstock.com

Money icon – pp.8, 134, 141, 142, 145 © LovArt/Shutterstock.com

Monochrome pattern – pp.32, 87, 143 © Zanna Pesnina/Shutterstock.com

Multi-colour strip background – pp.11, 28, 51, 80, 110, 140, 156 © Luxcor/Shutterstock.com

Pink geometric pattern – pp.57, 107 © RODINA OLENA/Shutterstock.com

Social icon – pp.8, 82, 85, 86, 89 © musmellow/Shutterstock.com

Speech bubble icon – pp.8, 62, 64, 94, 97, 98, 101, 105, 106, 109, 150 © LINE ICONS/Shutterstock.com

Speech mark and line design – pp.23, 84, 100, 114, 133 © CkyBe/Shutterstock.com

Thumbs down icon – pp.8, 45, 47, 49, 50, 56, 59, 60 © D Line/Shutterstock.com

Thumbs up icon – pp.8, 153 © RealVector/Shutterstock.com

Triangles – pp.4, 5, 7, 18, 20, 21, 38, 42, 52, 53, 62, 66, 67, 78, 79, 90–92, 102, 103, 121–123, 126, 127, 135–137, 146–148, 154, 155, 159 © Luci Ward